Copyright © Atsons Travel Guides

All rights reserved. Without limiting the above, no part of this publication may be into a retrieval system or transmitted in a (electronic, mechanical, photocopying or written permission of the copyright owner Guide.

We have relied on our own experience as well as many different sources for this Travel Guide, and we have done our best to check facts and to give credit where it is due. In the event that any material is incorrect or has been used without proper permission, please contact us so that the oversight can be corrected.

Written by: Shea Robinson

Edited by: Bruno Luis

Contents

Introduction to Amsterdam	3
#1 Anne Frank House	4
#2 Rijksmuseum	6
#3 Van Gogh Museum	8
#4 Vondelpark	10
#5 Jordaan	12
#6 Rembrandt House	14
#7 Heineken Experience	16
#8 The Resistance Museum	18
#9 Concertgebouw	20
#10 Museumplein	22
#11 Artis Royal Zoo	24
#12 Central Library	26
#13 Begijnhof	28
#14 Our Lord in the Attic	30
#15 Museum of Bags and Purses	32
#16 Centraal Station	34
#17 Red Light District	36
#18 Dam Square	38
#19 Stedelijk Museum	40
#20 National Maritime Museum	42
Map of all Attractions in Amsterdam	44

Introduction to Amsterdam

One of the greatest small cities in the world, Amsterdam is famous for many things – its canals, its Red Light District, its liberal attitude towards drugs, and its laid back atmosphere – however, it is also a city with countless cultural delights waiting to be discovered from world-class museums to historical buildings and fun attractions.

The city is one of the most tolerant and diverse in Europe which paves the way for an enticing nightlife, a rich culture, and the friendly attitude of a small village rather than a major European city.

There is so much to discover in Amsterdam it is hard to know where to start, although the transport hub of Centraal Station is as good of a starting place as any with trains, trams, and riverboats taking tourists and locals to all parts of the city.

The cultural side of Amsterdam is easy to discover with the Museumplein playing host to some of the country's best museums; the Rijksmuseum, the Van Gogh Museum, and the Stedelijk Museum as well as the wonderful Concertgebouw. There are plenty of other museums to discover in the city with none summing up the quirkiness of the Dutch more than the Museum of Bags and Purses.

The different districts of the city offer something unique and interesting from the once slum but now upper class district of Jordaan to the neon-lights of the Red Light District. Take in the atmosphere at Dam Square or escape the city in Vondelpark where events and entertainment is provided year-round.

The oppression once felt in this city can be seen in the Anne Frank House and the Our Lord in the Attic Museum, while there's plenty of fun to be had at the Heineken Experience and in the National Maritime Museum. Whichever way you choose to enjoy Amsterdam one thing is certain – this wonderful city will leave a lasting impression, and as soon as you leave you will no doubt be planning your return.

#1 Anne Frank House

© Wikimedia / Massimo Catarinella

Located in an unassuming building at the Prinsengracht, close to the Westerkerk, the Anne Frank House was the place of hiding for Anne Frank and her family for more than two years during the Second World War. Although Anne Frank didn't survive the war, her wartime diary was published in 1947, instantly becoming a worldwide bestseller, and in 1957 the Anne Frank Foundation was established to protect the property from developers who wanted to demolish the block.

Three years later, the house was converted into a museum, preserving the hiding place of Anne Frank, her family, and the two other families that hid there. Today it contains a permanent exhibition on the life and times of Anne Frank alongside an exhibition space about all forms of persecution and discrimination.

The house itself was constructed in 1635 by Dirk van Delft, with the canal facing façade renovated in 1740 after the rear annex of the building was demolished. The building originally acted as a private residence before finding purpose as a warehouse and in the 19th Century, the front warehouse was used to house horses.

At the beginning of the 20th Century, the building was occupied by a manufacturer of household appliances who was succeeded by a producer of piano rolls in 1930. The warehouse was vacated in 1939 and the following year Otto Frank, Anne's father, moved the offices of the spice and gelling companies he worked for, Opekta and Pectacon, from an address on Singel canal to Prinsengracht.

The Secret Annex, an extension at the rear of the building, was concealed from view by houses on all sides and made an ideal hiding place for Otto Frank, his wife Edith, two daughters (including Anne), and four other Jews seeking refuge from Nazi persecution.

The total floor space of the inhabited rooms came to only 46 square metres and all eight people remained hidden there for two years and one month until they were anonymously betrayed to the Nazi authorities, arrested, and deported to concentration camps. Of all the people hidden in the Secret Annex, only Otto survived in the concentration death camps.

After the arrests of those in hiding, the arresting officers cleared the hiding place of all remaining contents except a handful of items, including the Diary of Anne Frank, which were rescued by Miep Gies and Bep Voskuijl, who had helped hide the families.

© Wikimedia / Bungle

The Movable Bookcase that Covered the Entrance to the Annex

Upon the publication of the diary, the former hiding place of Anne Frank attracted a huge amount of interest with over 9,000 visitors arriving upon its opening to the public in 1960. Today, there is a range of original objects on display, a multimedia experience, a bookshop, and a café housed within the building.

The Anne Frank House costs €9 for adults and €4.50 for children 10 to 17 years old. Opening times are 9am to 7pm – 10pm (depending on season).

Address: Prinsengracht 263-267, 1016 GV Amsterdam, Netherlands

#2 Rijksmuseum

© Flickr / Dennis Jarvis

Located in the Museum Square, the Rijksmuseum (meaning State Museum) is dedicated to history and arts in Amsterdam. The museum is over 200 years old, opening its doors on 31 May 1800 as the Amsterdam National Art Gallery in The Hague and following the French example of the Louvre. Just six years later, the Kingdom of Holland was established by Napoleon Bonaparte and on the orders of his brother, Louis, the museum was moved to Amsterdam in 1808.

The museum opened its doors to the public in Amsterdam the following year in the Royal Palace before moving to the Trippenhuis in 1817 which was deemed unsuitable shortly after. In 1820 the historical objects of the museum were moved to the Mauritshuis in The Hague and in 1938 the 19th Century paintings were moved to Paviljoen Welgelegen in Haarlem.

The museum finally gained a permanent home when a competition to design a building was won by Pierre Cuypers in 1876. Nine years later, the Rijksmuseum was opened in its new, and current, location with a new building added in 1890 becoming the south wing or the Philips wing as it is known today.

The building consists of two squares with an atrium in each centre and a tunnel in the central axis with entrances at ground level and the Gallery of Honour on the first floor.

The architectural style is a Dutch neo-Renaissance with historical neo-Gothic elements in its decoration. In 1970 the building was declared a National Heritage Site and listed in the Top 100 Dutch Heritage Sites in 1990. Today, the collection consists of one million objects covering arts, crafts, and history from the beginning of the 13th Century to the turn of the millennium.

Within the collection is more than 2,000 paintings from the Dutch Golden Age by a host of notable painters, with highlights including; 'Portrait of a Young Couple' by Frans Hals, 'Jeremiah Lamenting the Destruction of Jerusalem' by Rembrandt, 'The Night Watch' by Rembrandt, 'The Milkmaid' by Johannes Vermeer, and 'Girl in a Blue Dress' by Johannes Cornelisz Verspronck.

© Wikimedia / Hajotthu

Interior of the Museum

There are two themed paths through the museum which can be explored – Dutch History which begins in 1506 with the Netherlands under Charles V and finishes with the Netherlands today, and Historical Figures which explores the lives of influential figures in Dutch history such as William of Orange, Piet Heyn, William II, and Louis Napoleon Bonaparte. The museum also has a small Asian collection which can be found in the Asian pavilion.

The Rijksmuseum costs €17.50 for adults and is free for visitors under 18 years old. Opening times are 9am to 5pm every day.

Address: Museumstraat 1, 1071 XX Amsterdam, Netherlands

#3 Van Gogh Museum

© Wikimedia / Wladyslaw

Home to the world's largest collection of works by Vincent Van Gogh and his contemporaries, the Van Gogh Museum houses a range of items including paintings, letters, and drawings by the famous Dutch painter as well as a collection of art from his contemporaries. Located at the Museum Square alongside other famous museums in Amsterdam, the Van Gogh Museum was opened in 1973 to provide a permanent home for the artist's collection.

Upon his death in 1890, Van Gogh's unsold works transferred into the possession of his brother Theo. Theo died only six months later and the collection was left to his widow, Johanna van Gogh-Bonger, who sold many paintings with the ambition of spreading knowledge about his artwork.

However, she also maintained a private collection of his works which was inherited by her son, Vincent Willem van Gogh, who in turn loaned the collection to the Stedlijk Museum. The collection was displayed in the Stedlijk for many years until it was transferred to the state-initiated Vincent van Gogh Foundation in 1962 who commissioned a design for a Van Gogh Museum a year later.

The design chosen for the museum was by Dutch architect Gerrit Rietveld, who unfortunately died a year after, meaning construction wasn't completed until 1973, the same year the museum opened its doors to the public. The building was renovated in 1998 and 1999 and again in 2012 during which time works were displayed in the Hermitage Amsterdam.

In 2013, the Van Gogh Museum unveiled a long-lost painting that had spent years in a Norwegian attic, the first full-size canvas by van Gogh discovered since 1928. 'Sunset at Montmajour' can be dated to the exact day it was painted, 4 July 1888, as it was described in a letter to his brother Theo.

The museum consists of two buildings; the Rietveld building and the Kurokawa wing. The Rietveld building is the main structure of the museum and houses the permanent collection over four floors. On the ground floor is a shop, café, and an introduction to the exhibition followed by works by van Gogh on the first floor ordered chronologically. The second floor displays information about the restoration of paintings and houses temporary exhibits, while the third floor shows paintings of van Gogh's contemporaries.

© Flickr / Minke Wagenaar

Interior of the Museum

The Kurokawa wing is used to house major temporary exhibitions over three floors, information of which can be found on the official website. Among the highlights in the museum are; 'Avenue of Poplars in Autumn', 'Wheat Field with a Lark', 'Sunflowers', 'The Yellow House', Almond Blossoms', and 'Wheatfield with Crows'. There are also some notable paintings by his contemporaries such as Maurice Denis, Claude Monet, Georges Seurat, Paul Signac, and Henri de Toulouse-Lautrec.

The Van Gogh Museum costs €17 for adults and is free for visitors up to 17 years old. Opening times are 9am to 5pm – 6pm every day and 9pm – 10pm on Fridays (depending on season).

Address: Paulus Potterstraat 7, 1071 CX Amsterdam, Netherlands

#4 Vondelpark

© Flickr / Barbara Walsh

The most famous park in the Netherlands and the largest city park in Amsterdam, Vondelpark is as vital to the city as the canals and coffee shops on a sunny day.

Located centrally, near to Museum Square and just south of Leidseplein, Vondelpark is always bustling with people enjoying the sun, taking the dog for a walk, roller-skating, listening to music, relaxing under the trees, or just lazing on the grass people-watching.

In the summer, free concerts are performed at the park's bandstand or in the open-air theatre, and numerous attractions throughout the park such as the statue of the poet Vondel, the cast iron music dome, the Groot Melkhuis complete with a playground for the children, and the historical Pavilion and restaurant ensure there is always something going on.

The park dates back to 1864, when a committee was formed by a group of prominent Amsterdam citizens who wished to create a public space. They raised money and purchased 8 hectares of land, commissioning landscape architect Jan David Zocher to design the park in the then fashionable English landscape style.

Zocher worked with his son Louis Paul Zocher using vistas, ponds, and pathways to create the illusion of a natural space. In 1865 the park was opened to the public as a horseback riding and strolling park called 'Nieuwe Park'. The name Vondelpark was adopted in 1867 when a statue of the Dutch poet was placed in the park.

The committee continued to raise money and by 1877, the park was enlarged to its current 45 hectares. At the time, it was situated at the edge of the city, however, today it has become part of the city centre with a prime location close to Museum Square and Leidseplein.

The position of the park on a muddy dump area means that it has to undergo complete renovation every 30 years. This is due to the ground lowering itself and if work was not completed it would be completely covered by water and endanger the foundations of nearby buildings. However, this wetland is ideal for a number of plants and trees such as Dutch red chestnuts, catalpas, and various birch trees as well as a variety of birds such as blue herons and ducks.

© Wikimedia / Henkgron

The Monument of Vondel

There are three main sculptures in Vondelpark; the three metre high bronze monument of Vondel by Louis Royer, the abstract concrete 'Fish' by Pablo Picasso, and the bronze Caribbean woman called 'Mama Baranka' by Nelson Carillho.

The park is also an ideal destination for families with small children as it contains six play areas and one large playground. On Queensday, the park becomes a Kinder Market where only children are allowed to trade.

#5 Jordaan

© Flickr / Per Salomonsson

Built as part of the large expansion of Amsterdam in the early 17th Century, Jordaan was characterised as a district for the working class and immigrants to the city.

In the following centuries, the population of the district dramatically increased, mainly due to a steady stream of political refugees such as protestant Fleming, Spanish, and Portuguese Jews. The area became a kind of ghetto in the city with small houses, slums, and families cramped into tiny rooms with lots of children.

The area had open sewers, with the canals serving as both a means of transport and a sewer, and had no running water with the population reaching around 80,000 at the turn of the 20th Century in comparison to just 20,000 today. The area had many famous residents such as the 17th Century Dutch writer Joost van den Vondel and photographer Breitner as well as Rembrandt during his later years.

During the 20th Century, the council had plans to demolish large parts of the district and construct bland blocks of modern buildings. However, the residents of Jordaan protested against this idea and groups such as Monument Care were set up to protect the historical value of the area. Thanks to these protests, the plan was modified and instead works were carried out on a small scale to repair neighbourhoods while maintaining their original character.

By the time the renovations had begun, Jordaan had been discovered by a new generation of occupants; artists, young entrepreneurs, and students. The older inhabitants gradually moved to other neighbourhoods or cities such as Almere and the district slowly changed from a slum area to a rich and artistic area.

Today, Jordaan is considered an oasis from the rest of the city with narrow streets, art studios, trickling canals, wonderful courtyards, old-fashioned pubs, and high-end boutiques.

The area is also famous for its markets such as Lindenmarkt which is open every Saturday and Noordermarkt which is a flea market on Mondays and a biological food market for the rest of the week. Beside Noordermarkt is the main church of Jordaan, Nooderkerk, which was built in the early 17th Century and is still used as a protestant church today. The other main church of the area is Westerkerk which features a wonderful West Tower that can be seen from most angles in the neighbourhood.

© Wikimedia / kevinmcgill

Canal in Jordaan

Many of the museums in the area are quite small with the highlights including the Pianola Museum with old mechanical pianos, the Theo Thijssen literate Museum, and a fluorescent museum called Electric Lady Land. There is also a Jordaan Museum which is dedicated to the history of the district.

#6 Rembrandt House

© Wikimedia / Michiel1972

Found near the Chinese Quarter of Amsterdam near the famous Red Light District, the Rembrandt House is the place where the famous artist lived between 1639 and 1660, when he went bankrupt and had to sell most of his possessions. A modern annex has been recently built next to the house which, along with the house, creates a museum of Rembrandt's life and work.

The museum is a fascinating insight into the life of the Dutch artist and reveals unknown aspects about his artistic craft. The interior of the house is reconstructed according to details of the painter's everyday life and, although lacking authenticity as with many reconstructions, still delves deep into the artist's psyche.

The building itself was constructed in 1606 and 1607 in what was then known as the Sint Anthonisbreestraat. The area was known for its wealth and prosperity, attracting a number of rich merchants and prosperous artists to the area.

In 1627-28 the house was remodelled and given a new façade along with another storey. It is likely that this work was carried out by Jocob van Campen, who was also responsible for the Amsterdam Town Hall.

After Rembrandt's occupation of the house it was altered several times and its condition slowly deteriorated, until the City of Amsterdam purchased it in 1907 leading to the restoration of the building and the opening of the museum in 1911.

The original collection consisted of a few etchings, however, as a result of gifts and purchases, the museum's collection grew steadily and today has an excellent collection consisting of works by Rembrandt and artists from his studio.

The home and studio section of the museum is reconstructed with works of furniture, art, and various other objects to demonstrate what it may have looked like during Rembrandt's tenancy. Throughout the museum is the world's most complete collection of Rembrandt's etchings with copperplates, landscapes, nudes, portraits, genre, self-portraits, and faces found hanging and on display.

Interior of the Museum

As well as the works by Rembrandt, the museum is home to a superb collection of paintings by artists known as Pre-Rembrandtists- painters who were working in Amsterdam before the great artist arrived in 1631. Among the highlights in this collection which inspired Rembrandt are 'The Crucifixion' and 'De bewning van Abel' by Pieter Lastman, 'The Expulsion of Hagar' by Jan Pynas, and 'Christ appearing to Mary Magdalene' by Ferdinand Bol.

The Rembrandt House costs €12.50 for adults and €4 for children aged 6 – 17. Opening times are 10am to 6pm every day.

Address: Jodenbreestraat 4, 1011 NK Amsterdam, Netherlands

#7 Heineken Experience

© Wikimedia / Mtcv

There has always been an air of secrecy surrounding the world's best beers and most certainly Heineken pilsner is part of that group. The historic brewery was established in Amsterdam in 1864 and has since become a multi-national company and one of the three largest producers of beer in the world.

Throughout its history, Heineken has by and large remained a family run company, with Charlene de Carvalho-Heineken as the largest stockholder and her husband, Michael, also on the company's board. The now defunct Amsterdam brewery has been remodelled to present visitors with information about the company's rich and successful history as well as adding several amusement park rides and renaming itself as the Heineken Experience.

When the Amsterdam brewery was closed by Heineken in 1988, the company decided to open a museum in its place, and in 1991 visitors could visit the old brewery, tour the building, learn about the famous pilsner, and drink as much as they like. Known as the 'Heineken Treat and Information Centre' it quickly grew to become one of Amsterdam's most popular attractions, and in 2001 rebranded itself as the Heineken Experience.

In 2008, the museum underwent an expensive expansion and remodelling, transforming the experience into a four level tour with historical artefacts, product exploration and sampling, and interactive exhibits with the latest high-tech multi-media technologies.

The museum part of the attraction is undoubtedly the highlight with the architecture of the 19th Century Heineken brewery buildings, authentic interior, old photographs, and state decorations received by the Heineken family on display, including a gold medal from the Universal Exhibition in Paris dating 1889. In fact, you may already recognise the gold medal which is reproduced on each can of Heineken as a symbol of the company.

The newer additions to the attraction are hit and miss with screenings of very old beer commercials, a quasi-3D movie, and actors swimming in pools of beer making up this section of the experience.

© Flickr / Phil Wiffen

Inside the Heineken Experience

However, the Heineken Experience is a fun afternoon out for all the family and the old brewery building acts as an anchor point on the European Route of Industrial Heritage which certainly makes it worth a visit.

The Heineken Experience costs €18 for adults and €12.50 for children aged 12 – 17. Opening times are 11am to 7.30pm – 8.30pm depending on the day and season.

Address: Stadhouderskade 78, 1072 AE Amsterdam, Netherlands

#8 The Resistance Museum

© Wikimedia / A. Bakker

Undoubtedly the best historical museum in the Netherlands, the Resistance Museum tells the story of the Dutch people in World War II, a time when the country was occupied by Nazi Germany.

Located in the Plantage neighbourhood, the museum, also known as Verzetsmuseum, came about when a group of different political streams who fought against the Nazi occupation during the Second World War worked together to construct an exhibition about their struggle called 1933-19nu.

1933 is in reference to the year Hitler took power in Germany and the translation of 19nu is 19now. The growing feeling among the Dutch public that this period of history should be given special attention led to the exhibition becoming a permanent museum and the Resistance Museum was established in 1984.

The building bearing the Star of David and the name of Petrus Plancius, the Renaissance Amsterdam clergyman and geographer who lived from 1550 to 1622, had already been built in 1876 by the Jewish singing society, Oefening Baart Kunst.

It has served for several decades as a synagogue and a Jewish cultural centre, with the name of Petrus Plancius purposefully kept on the building by the Oefening baart Kunst society to underline their respect for Amsterdam traditions.

The building served many purposes before becoming the permanent home for the Resistance Museum. Although the museum is quite small, it is a fascinating place to visit and a far cry from the doom and gloom of many other war museums.

The permanent exhibition of the museum recreates the atmosphere of the streets of Amsterdam during the German occupation of the city in the Second World War. Large photographs, old propaganda posters, various objects, grainy films, and sound effects all combine to create a dramatic scene within the museum.

The background of the Holocaust is visually represented to visitors through the lives of everyday people at the time. The stories of resistance against the Nazi invasion and of individual heroes makes this museum a memorable experience. The museum also houses a pleasant café and restaurant on the ground floor and is highly recommended when combined with the Anne Frank Museum.

© Wikimedia / Cezary p

Interior of the Museum

The Resistance Museum costs €8 for adults and €4.50 for children aged 7 – 15. Opening times are 10am/12pm to 5pm depending on the day of the week.

Address: Plantage Kerklaan 61A, 1018 CX Amsterdam, Netherlands

#9 Concertgebouw

© Wikimedia / Cha già José

Located on Museum Square, Concertgebouw literally translates as 'Concert Building' and is home to the Royal Concertgebouw Orchestra, the Dutch Philharmonic Orchestra, and the Dutch Chamber Orchestra. In 2013, on the building's 125th anniversary, Queen Beatrix bestowed the royal title of 'Koninklijk' upon the building, as she had done previously with the Royal Concertgebouw Orchestra.

The highly regarded acoustics in the building means it is regarded as one of the three finest concert halls in the world alongside Boston's Symphony Hall and the Musikverein in Vienna. A modern annex on the building allows it to have space for a large booking office and a grand reception area for guests.

The construction of the building was completed in 1886, however, it didn't open until two years later with an inaugural concert conducted by Henri Viotta on 11 April 1888 with 120 musicians and 500 singers participating. Between 1982 and 1995, the whole building was restored when it was found to be slowly sinking into the ground and a modern annex was added to the original hall.

The Main Hall seats 1,974 and stretches 44 metres long and 28 metres wide with a height of 17 metres. The reverberation time is 2.8 seconds without an audience and 2.2 seconds with an audience, making it ideal for the late Romantic repertoire such as Mahler.

Beside the Main Hall is the smaller, oval-shaped venue, the Recital Hall which measures 20 metres long and 15 metres wide. The more intimate space here is perfectly suited to chamber music.

Today, Concertgebouw hosts some 900 concerts and other events per year with over 700,000 annual visitors, making it one of the most visited concert halls in the world. The concerts are split between the Main Hall and the Recital Hall and cover a broad spectrum of music including classical concerts, jazz, pop, and special events such as congresses and festive occasions.

Classical music concerts are organised in several traditional series; the Robeco Summer Concerts, the Sunday Morning Concerts, the Saturday Matinee Concerts, and the Wednesday Lunch Concerts. Prior to all Sunday Morning concerts it is possible to visit the building, go behind the scenes, and enjoy a private tour with detailed information about the building and the orchestra.

© Wikimedia / FaceMePLS

The Concert Hall

During the summer months the tours are also available prior to the Robeco Summer Concerts. Among the highlights of the tour is the organ which was built in 1890 and has 60 registers on three divisions and pedal.

Concertgebouw concert tickets start at €14.50 with free concerts held every Wednesday lunchtime. Guided tours must be booked in advance and cost €10 per person. Guided Tours are held in English every Sunday between 12.30pm and 1.45pm.

Address: Concertgebouwplein 10, 1071 LN Amsterdam, Netherlands

#10 Museumplein

© Flickr / FaceMePLS

Home to three of Amsterdam's most famous museums and the Concertgebouw, Museumplein or 'Museum Square' was created to host the World Exhibition in 1883. However, it only gained its lasting title when the Rijksmuseum opened on the square two years later.

Numerous facelifts and reconstructions have occurred at Museumplein over the years such as the raising of a triangle of turf at the southern end, dubbed the 'ass's ear' for its shape, which is now a popular spot for sun bathing and picnicking.

This reconstruction in 1999 also created an underground parking lot and an underground supermarket with the pond transforming into an artificial ice skating area in the winter.

The area is the pinnacle of sophistication in Amsterdam thanks to its wealth of cultural landmarks beginning with the Concertgebouw on Van Baarlestraat which has stood on the same spot since 1888. If you don't get a chance to enjoy a concert inside the world famous acoustic halls, you might be in luck as the orchestra occasionally hold concerts outside the building, especially in the summer months.

Moving past the Concertgebouw is the Museum Quarter which is considered by many to be the central hub of the city.

Strolling down the exclusive P.C. Hooftstraat, Pieter Cornelisz, or Van Baerlesstraat will reveal some of the most chic couture houses Amsterdam has to offer. From diamonds to leather shoes and designer handbags, any shopaholic will feel right at home along these streets.

Museumplein also caters very well for families with children and offers a public skateboard park and a wading pool which doubles as an ice rink in winter.

After stopping in to observe the best art and culture that Amsterdam has to offer in the Rijksmuseum, the Van Gogh Museum, and the Stedelijk Museum, the wide open spaces of Vondelpark are only a stone's throw away.

© Flickr / keriluamox

Concertgebouw in Museumplein

Depending on the time of year, Vondelpark is the perfect place for a relaxing stroll, a spot of lunch, or celebrations if it is King's Day or Uitmarkt.

The Museum Quarter is also a popular location for mass events such as festivals, celebrations, and demonstrations with the Dutch football team often meeting the fans after a major tournament here.

#11 Artis Royal Zoo

© Wikimedia / Jvhertum

Founded in 1838, the Artis Royal Zoo (Artis being short for 'Natura Artis Magistra' which is Latin for 'Nature is the teacher of art and science') remains as enchanting today as it was when it first opened. Artis Royal Zoo isn't just a zoo, it is also an aquarium, a planetarium, and contains an arboretum and a large art collection.

It is also one of the few zoos in Europe to have a huge number of listed buildings; the Large Museum, the Library Building, and the Aquarium among them. When the zoo was founded in 1838 it was initially open only to members. In 1851 it was opened to the public for the first time in the month of September, and in 1920 it became open to the public all year round.

There are several sections to Artis, many of which are contained within the historic buildings. The Aquarium features a vast diversity of underwater life with enormous aquatic tanks in the Main Hall leading through to replicas of the

Amazonian rainforest, the tropical coral reef, and the authentic Amsterdam canal.

The Butterfly Pavilion is the largest of its kind in the Netherlands and covers a total of 1,000 square metres, housing thousands of butterflies.

Depending on the season, the Butterfly Pavilion boasts dozens of species including the Blue Morpho and the Swallowtail Butterfly. Twice a day, butterflies that have just crawled out of their cocoons are released into the pavilion. The Insectarium was converted from a food storage facility in 2005 and boasts a huge range of insects to discover.

A great way to learn about the wealth of animals kept in Artis Zoo is to attend a zookeeper talk or take a guided tour, details of both can be found in the information centre upon arrival.

The talks take place at various enclosures around the zoo at specific times including the vulture talk which demonstrates the bird's huge wings and how they pick their cadavers clean, the red ruffed lemurs talk which allows visitors to stand among them, the lion talk which coincides with their feeding time, the giant tortoise talk which allows guests to touch their shell, the penguin talk which occurs at feeding time, and the Japanese macaques talk which is held on Monkey Island.

© Flickr / Martin Fisch

Ankole-Watusi at the Artis Royal Zoo

The Planetarium is also worth a visit while in the zoo and allows visitors to experience the universe by whizzing through space. Finally, be sure to take a stroll in the magnificent Botanical Gardens which have an excellent diversity of plants and trees.

Artis Royal Zoo costs €19.95 for adults and €16.50 for children ages 3 – 9. Opening times are 9am to 5pm or 6pm (depending on season).

Address: Plantage Kerklaan 38-40, 1018 CZ Amsterdam, Netherlands

#12 Central Library

© Wikimedia / Gkamiya

The largest of Amsterdam's 28 public libraries and 43 lending points which are collectively known as the Openbare Bilbliotheek Amsterdam, the Central Library moved to its current location at the Oosterdokseiland east of Amsterdam Central Station in 2007 after being located at the Prinsengracht for 30 years.

The enormous complex has a floor space of 28,500 metres squared spread out over ten floors with 1,200 seats and 600 internet-connected computers managed by 200 staff. Said to be the largest library in Europe, it also consists of a theatre, a radio station, conference rooms, an exhibition space, a music department, study pods, a reader's café, and a restaurant with an outdoor terrace overlooking the city.

The concept behind the €80 million library was as a cultural centre that promotes education, reading, and understanding among all sectors of society. The architect, Jo Coenen, who was also responsible for the nearby KNSM Island and the Central Library of Maastricht, was challenged to increase the time people spent in the library. The authorities wanted people to spend longer than the average 20 minutes inside the building and for it to act as not just a book store but a learning centre and a site of expression and entertainment.

Coenen achieved this through focusing his work on both natural and artificial light which can be seen by the large windows used on the design. As well as designing and creating the lighting design for the building, Coenen designed a system for distributing fresh air throughout the building which cools it by drawing cold air from outside.

Once you enter the building, large white panels that illuminate the stairs contain black letters which indicate what can be found on each floor. The basement is devoted to children and contains small buildings in the form of towers with which they can be entertained while reading their favourite books.

The ground floor contains a selection of magazines and newspapers alongside the reader's café, and visitors can also bring books up to the restaurant on the 8th floor to enjoy the stunning view from the roof terrace.

© Wikimedia / Ceinturion

Inside the Library

There are lots of spaces to be discovered in the library such as a space at the rear of the 5th floor which contains 15 chairs and acts as a relaxation area.

The Theatre of the Word is also located within the building and, with a capacity of 270 people, plays host to concerts, plays, and documentary screenings. Visitors can also watch as radio stations Amsterdam FM and OBA Live broadcast live from the first floor and fourth floor respectively.

The Central Library is free to enter. Opening times are 10am to 10pm every day.

Address: Oosterdoksstraat 143, 1011 DL Amsterdam, Netherlands

#13 Begijnhof

© Flickr / Dennis Jarvis

An enclosed courtyard dating from the early 14th Century, the Begijnhof was originally built as a sanctuary for the Begijntjes, a Catholic sisterhood who lived like nuns, but today is the site of the English Reformed Church.

The Begijnhof is the only inner courtyard in the city that was founded during the Middle Ages and therefore lies within the Singel, the innermost canal of Amsterdam's circular canal system, and is at Medieval street level which is one metre below the rest of the old city centre.

The courtyard was originally completely encircled by water with a sole entrance located at the Begijnensteeg which had a bridge across the Begijnensloot. The current Spui entrance only dates back to the 19th Century.

After the Alteration (Protestant takeover) in 1578, when Amsterdam came under Calvinist rule, the Begijnhof was the only Roman Catholic institution allowed to remain in existence because the houses around the courtyard were the Begijntjes' private property. However, the chapel was closed and lay derelict for around 30 years before being ceded to the English Presbyterians and since then has become known as the 'English Church'.

In 1671, architect Philip Vingboons converted two dwellings located directly opposite the Chapel's entrance into a conventicle church for Catholics, the Church of the Saints John and Ursula, named after the patron saints of the Begijnhof.

This church was kept secret and was not recognised as a church outside the courtyard until it became the Miracle Church in 1908 after the original Miracle Church had been deliberately destroyed by its Protestant owners.

The buildings that surround the courtyard are tall and typically Amsterdam-style townhouses, emphasising the court's relatively private character. Unlike most courts, the houses don't form rows joining one dwelling with another, but instead contains 47 regular townhouses, each with its own individual features.

© Flickr / Ashwin Chandrasekaran

Statue of Christ

The majority of the buildings still feature Gothic wooden framework with 17th or 18th Century façades. The most famous of these is the so-called 'Wooden House' as it is only one of two wooden houses still standing in the city, dating from around 1528 it is also the oldest wooden house in Amsterdam.

Another feature of the Begijnhof is the Begijnesloot Gate which dates from 1574 and contains a gable stone depicting Saint Ursula. When visiting the Begijnhof, bear in mind that the houses are still occupied and visitors are asked to respect their privacy.

#14 Our Lord in the Attic

© Flickr / Gary Ullah

Previously called Museum Amstelkring, Our Lord in the Attic is among the most cherished museums in the city. The attic of this house, which appears like any other house from the outside, was used as clandestine church for Catholic worshipers who were unable to worship in public during the 17th Century.

Since the late 19th Century, the canal house has been opened as a museum and contains a collection of church silver along with various religious artefacts and paintings. The history of the clandestine church is what makes a visit so fascinating with the story dating back to the Alteration (Protestant takeover) of 1578, when Catholics were no longer able to worship in public.

In 1661, a wealthy Catholic merchant named Jan Hartman bought a stately canal house along with the two houses directly behind it. He was a devout man who made the decision to include a Catholic chapel in his new property with the rest of the house being used as living space for his family, storage, and as a reception area for guests. The hidden chapel occupied the entire top floor of the canal house and the two houses directly behind it, and would end up serving as the parish church for Catholics in the area for 200 years.

The church was affectionately known as 'the Hart', inspired by the host's name, and was dedicated to St. Nicholas. In 1739, the chapel underwent renovations after it was purchased by the priest, Ludovicus Reiniers, who added another stairway, rebuilt the façade, and began referring to the chapel as 'Our Lord in the Attic'.

When visiting Our Lord in the Attic, guests can access the chapel on the top floor by old, creaky, steep wooden stairs. The long nave of the chapel is lined with two wooden galleries and still contains seating for around 150 worshippers along with some fine paintings and sculptures. The decoration is in the Dutch Classicist style and features marble columns, gilded capitals, and stucco sculptures of God and the Holy Spirit.

As well as the chapel, guests are able to explore the rest of this fascinating house which is wonderfully preserved in its original 17th Century condition. The house includes a variety of rooms such as the kitchen which is decorated with painted porcelain tiles, a chaplain bedroom with period furnishings, a storeroom on the ground floor, and a wonderful drawing room on the first floor.

© Wikimedia / PMRMaeyaert

Our Lord in the Attic

The drawing room is the star attraction of the rest of the house and was designed to impress guests with stately furnishings and artwork such as a copy of Andrea Schiavone's 'Presentation of Jesus in the Temple'.

Our Lord in the Attic costs €6 for adults and €4 for children ages 5 – 18. Opening times are 10am to 5pm daily, except Sundays when the attraction opens at 1pm.

Address: Oudezijds Voorburgwal 40, 1012 GE Amsterdam, Netherlands

#15 Museum of Bags and Purses

© Wikimedia / Marion Golsteijn

One of only three museums in the world that specialise in the field and the largest collection of its kind in the world, the Museum of Bags and Purses is certainly a unique attraction. The idea for the museum arose in the 1980s, when antique dealer Hendrikje Ivo from Amstelveen purchased a small antique tortoiseshell bag inlaid with mother of pearl in England which was crafted in Germany and dated back to 1820.

Ivo's interest in uncovering the history of the bag triggered a passion for collecting handbags, and before long she had amassed a collection numbering over 3,000. At first, the museum existed in a small two room villa in Amstelveen, however, as the collection grew she began looking for a new location.

In June 2007, the museum relocated to a beautiful 17th Century partisan house at the Herengracht, along

Amsterdam's most prestigious canal. Today, the museum has grown into a serious institution with a huge permanent collection that displays the core of the collection along with a rotating temporary exhibition displaying particular designers, most of whom are Dutch.

Additionally, the exhibition has been completed by 150 fans from the collection created by another avid collector, Felix Tal. Upon the opening of the new museum, Hendrikje Ivo was knighted in appreciation of her merits to the Dutch culture. This incredible museum has a luxurious feel when visiting, centred as it is on only one object. Visitors often remark how upon being admitted into the museum, they feel like they are entering the private reception of an important fashion show in Paris.

The permanent collection's earliest handbags are typically small and used to carry coins, sewing kits, and keys. Such bags would have been used by both men and women, carried under an overcoat to avoid the attention of thieves. The development of pockets in men's pants and the change from billowing skirts to more form-fitting dresses for women, led to handbags becoming an item almost exclusively for women.

© Flickr / bert knottenbeld

Collection of Bags

Upon the arrival of the Industrial Revolution in the 18th Century, the rise in rail travel led to handbags becoming larger and more durable, often made of leather.

Brand names made their arrival on the scene in the 1950s, epitomised by items in the collection such as a quilted Chanel purse and a Hermes Kelly bag. The temporary exhibitions generally run for two to five months and feature themes such as 'Crystal loves Leather' and 'Happy Birthday Chanel'.

The Museum of Bags and Purses costs €9 for adults and €6 for children ages 13 – 18. Opening times are 10am to 5pm daily.

Address: Herengracht 573, 1017 CD Amsterdam, Netherlands

#16 Centraal Station

© Wikimedia / jimmyweee

Amsterdam's main train station is the true heart of the city. Central not only in name, but also serving as the biggest public transfer spot with over 250,000 people passing through the station every day. It is the location of the final stop for several lines of city tram and buses as well as the waterfront station for city ferry lines that take cars and passengers to Amsterdam North.

It is also the location of the main Amsterdam Tourist Office and the departure point for river cruises and sightseeing boats along the city's canals. The building is listed as a National Heritage Site and as such is the most visited site of such status in the country.

The station was designed by Pierre Cuypers, who is also known for his design of the Rijksmuseum on Museumplein. While he is listed as the main architect, it is likely that he was mainly responsible for the decoration and railway engineers were in charge of the structural design.

Centraal Station replaced Amsterdam Willemspoort Station which had closed in 1878, as well as the temporary Westerdok Station which was used from 1878 to 1889. The idea for Centraal Station came from Johan Rudolph Thorbecke, the then Netherlands Minister for the National Railways, who had laid the idea before the Amsterdam municipal council in 1884.

The design of the station by Cuypers strongly resembled his design of the Rijksmuseum, of which construction had begun two years previous. It features a palace-like Gothic Renaissance Revival façade with two turrets and various ornamental detail alongside stone reliefs in reference to the city's industrial and commercial importance.

Construction of the station began in 1882 with the foundations laid on three interconnected artificial islands in the IJ Lake. These islands were created with sand taken from the dunes near Velsen which were available due to the excavation of the North Sea Canal.

The instability of the soil held back construction for several years and although the building was completed in 1884, the station didn't officially open until 1889.

© Flickr / Riza Nugraha

Inside Centraal Station

The opening of the station marked the city's transition from a waterfront city to an inland city, spurring further development activities around the city centre and eventually leading to the canals being replaced by tramways and cars as the primary modes of transport.

Today, the station is the hub of all transport in the city as well as providing fast train connections to other major European cities such as Paris and Cologne.

Address: Stationsplein, 1012 AB Amsterdam, Netherlands

#17 Red Light District

© Wikimedia / Vvlasenko

From brothels to one-roomed cabins rented by prostitutes to museums, the Red Light District in Amsterdam leaves nothing to the imagination. World famous, it is likely that visitors to Amsterdam have already heard rumours or stories about this area, and while most of it is probably true it is worthwhile taking a stroll through the streets to find out the facts for yourself.

Known by the locals as the 'Rossebuurt', it is a place unlike anywhere else with images posted around the world of women of all nationalities parading their wares in red-fringed windows and of packs of men, women, and couples pointing in the shock of it all. The Red Light District is also known for one of Amsterdam's other famous institutions – the coffee shops that sell marijuana.

The history of the area dates back to the 13th Century when a bridge was built across the river at Dam Square where the Rokin and Damrak meet. The Damrak became a harbour due to this bridge and it is there where the Red Light District first appeared. Historically, because of its proximity to the harbour, the area attracted both prostitution and migrant populations with working girls often venturing out at night to the pubs and inns to pick up clients.

In the 18th Century, wealthy men would meet working girls at gambling houses, leading to the gambling houses providing board for the girls and investing in luxurious furnishings to attract more wealthy men. Over time, these houses became brothels employing up to 30 girls, and although prostitution was tolerated at this time it didn't become legal until 1811.

Due to religious organisations running campaigns in the early 20th Century, brothels and pimping was banned in 1911 and the working girls were forced underground. Today, prostitution is legal with the exception of street prostitution.

As one of Amsterdam's foremost attractions, there are several agencies that offer guided tours of the Red Light District. Embarking on one of these tours is highly recommended as it shows the area in a whole new way.

The Red Light District, although famous for its prostitution, is one of the most beautiful parts of the city with long winding cobbled streets and charming 14th Century architecture such as the Gothic Oude Kerk or Old Church.

© Flickr / Qiou87

Red Light District at Dusk

Recent transformations in the area including the resurfacing of the streets, restored façades, and the opening of classier eateries has altered a once seedy area into a safe and friendly environment.

If you are seeking a bit more culture than sex shops, window prostitutes, and cannabis cafés, the picturesque Zeedijk, Jewish Quarter, Waterloo Square, and Nieuwmarkt are all just around the corner, as is the wonderfully colourful Chinatown area.

#18 Dam Square

© Wikimedia / Coenvanderwoude

Located just five minutes from Centraal Station, Dam Square is the main plaza in Amsterdam, packed with attractions and bustling with people both day and night. Created in the 13th Century when a dam was built around the river Amstel to prevent the Zuiderzee Sea from overflowing and swarming the city, the square has been an important location throughout history.

The most famous event to occur on Dam Square was on 7 May 1945, two days after German capitulation in the Second World War when thousands of Dutch people were waiting for Canadian troops to arrive.

As the people danced and sang, the Germans placed a machine gun on the balcony and starting randomly firing into the crowds. The motives behind the shooting remains unclear, however, 120 people were seriously injured and 22 pronounced dead once the mayhem had finished.

Today, the square contains a number of food stalls, restaurants, and shops, including the trendy Bijenkorf, Magna Plaza, Bonneterie, and the Amsterdam Diamond Centre. The square is so popular that it isn't unusual to have to wait for a seat at one of the cafés or restaurants, especially in the evenings or at the weekend.

There are plenty of events that take place on the square throughout the year such as carnivals in the spring, street performers in the summer, and a funfair around Christmas time and King's Day.

On the 4 May every year, the square is the focus point for the celebrations of National Memorial Day. It is also the meeting point of several tram lines, and before the construction of Centraal Station was the most important tram hub of the city.

Of all the attractions in and around Dam Square, the Royal Palace is quite literally the jewel in the crown. Although it is no longer the residence of the Dutch Royal family, the grand 17th Century palace is still used to host official receptions.

Opposite the Royal Palace is the National Monument statue, erected in memory of Dutch soldiers and members of the resistance who died in the Second World War. Unveiled in 1956, the monument stores soil from all of Holland's provinces as well as from the Dutch East Indies and is somewhat controversial due to its phallic shape.

© Wikimedia / Jorge Royan

The National Monument

Other must-sees in the square include Madame Tussauds, the famous wax work museum, the New Church, often home to art exhibitions, and Beurs van Berlage, an old stock exchange building which is now used as a concert hall.

#19 Stedelijk Museum

© Wikimedia / Editør

Located on Museum Square, the Stedelijk Museum, colloquially known as Stedelijk, strives to be one of the most innovative museums of modern art in the world.

The collection is vast and consists of modern and contemporary art and design from the 20th and 21st Centuries with artists such as Vincent Van Gogh, Ernst Ludwig Kirchner, Karel Appel, Willem de Kooning, and Andy Warhol on display.

The museum opened in 1895 as part of an initiative of the local authority and private individuals as part of a modernisation project spearheaded by local citizens in 1850. The building was designed by Dutch architect Adriaan Willem Weissman in a Dutch Neo-Renaissance style and was largely funded by Sophia Adriana de Bruyn.

The original collection of the museum consisted mainly of militaria of the Amsterdam militia, Asiatic art, and artefacts from the

Museum of Chronology and the Medical-Pharmaceutical Museum. From 1930, the museum began actively acquiring art and the Museum of Applied Art opened on the ground floor in 1934 displaying a collection of art with emphasis on the Dutch work from the turn of the century.

After the Second World War, the museum began to acquire photography, making it the first western European museum for modern art to collect photographs. In 2008, the museum underwent a major construction, reopening its doors in 2010 with a program called 'The Temporary Stedelijk' in the unfinished historical building and reopening fully in 2012 with a new modern wing.

The museum collection holds around 90,000 objects which have been collected since 1874 and represent virtually every significant art movement throughout the 20th and 21st Centuries. The collection is subdivided into the following disciplines; Painting, Sculpture, Installation, Moving Image and Sound, Prints and Drawings, Posters, Photography, Graphic Design, Industrial Design, Artist Books, and Lucebert Archive.

The collection is considered one of the richest modern art collections in the world with all the important names of modern painting movements featured, as well as a unique collection of 29 paintings by Casimir Malevich, an exceptional collection of De Stijl and Cobra Movement, a fascinating collection of Dutch photography, and works by classic artists such as Matisse, Picasso, Newman, Rauschenberg, and Warhol.

© Flickr / Hans Griep

An Exhibition in the Museum

The museum also hosts a rage of modern arts events such as performances, films, lectures, and music concerts, details of which can be found on the official website.

The Stedelijk Museum costs €15 for adults and is free for children under 18. Opening times are 10am to 6pm daily and 11am – 10pm on Thursdays.

Address: Museumplein 10, 1071 DJ Amsterdam, Netherlands

#20 National Maritime Museum

© Wikimedia / S Sepp

The first of Amsterdam's major museums to open after an extensive renovation project in 2011, the National Maritime Museum is located near the city's old harbour in a wonderful historic building. The building is a former naval storehouse called Lands Zeemagazijn which was designed by Dutch architect Daniel Stalpaert and constructed in 1656. It was used as the main storehouse of the Amsterdam Admiralty until 1973 when it was converted into the ultra-modern Maritime Museum.

To construct the building, Stalpaert had to construct an artificial island created in Amsterdam harbour and 1,800 piles had to be sunk into the muddy ground for the foundations. During the recent renovations, a vast space of the building's inner courtyard has been covered by a glass dome which, in the evenings, lights up with thousands of tiny LEDs to create a starry sky effect.

Docked outside the museum is a replica of the three masted 'Amsterdam', a large vessel of the

Dutch East India Company which in its maiden journey sank in a storm in the English Channel in 1749. The wreck of the ship was discovered in 1969 and the museum replica was based entirely on the wreckage, being completed in 1990. Part of the museum experience is visiting the ship where you can see how small and primitive the spaces were that housed a crew of almost 350 people.

The permanent exhibition is enormous and would take several hours just to walk through. It is split into several themes to help finding the most personally interesting parts easy, with the highlights including; See You in the Golden Age, Port 24/7, Voyage at Sea, the Ship Decorations, and the Navigational Instruments.

The 'See You in the Golden Age' exhibition focuses on the prosperous period of the 17th Century with multimedia experiences bringing visitors up close and personal with characters who lived during this time. 'Port 24/7' explores the large port of Amsterdam and the huge variety of products that came in and out of the docks, as well as all the goings on via an exciting container ride.

The 'Voyage at Sea' section is a favourite among children as they embark on a virtual adventure at sea beginning 350 years ago in the Zeemagazijn, the very building that today houses the museum. As well as the interactive exhibitions there are some fascinating paintings dating from the 17th Century and ship decorations, also dating from the 17th Century on display.

© Flickr / Nigel Swales

A Replica of The Amsterdam Moored Next to the Museum

The museum provides a superb day out for anyone interested in understanding the history of the Dutch people in a unique way as well as providing lots of activities for families with children of any age.

The National Maritime Museum costs €15 for adults and €7.50 for children ages 5 - 17. Opening times are 9am to 5pm daily.

Address: Kattenburgerplein 1, 1018 KK Amsterdam, Netherlands

Map of all Attractions in Amsterdam

#1 Anne Frank House

#2 Rijksmuseum

#3 Van Gogh Museum

#4 Vondelpark

#5 Jordaan

#6 Rembrandt House

#7 Heineken Experience

#8 The Resistance Museum

#9 Concertgebouw

#10 Museumplein

#11 Artis Royal Zoo

#12 Central Library

#13 Begijnhof

#14 Our Lord in the Attic

#15 Museum of Bags and Purses

#16 Centraal Station

#17 Red Light District

#18 Dam Square

#19 Stedelijk Museum

#20 National Maritime Museum

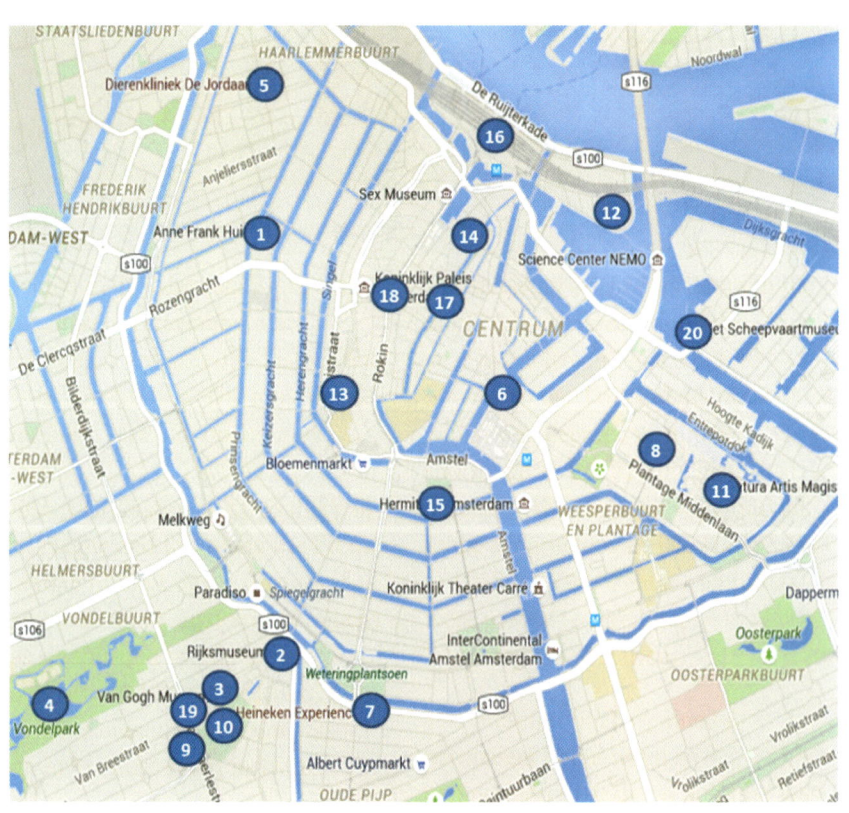

A Note to the Reader

Dear Reader

Thank you for your purchase of this Atsons Travel guide, we hope you have enjoyed reading it!

Please feel free to post an informative, unbiased review on Amazon so that others may benefit from your experience. A Review would be greatly appreciated as it helps us spread the word of our books and attract more fantastic customers such as yourselves.

Also your feedback is invaluable to us, as we work hard to serve you and continually improve our customers' experience.

Sincerely

Atsons Travel Guides

Printed in Great Britain
by Amazon